ACKNOWLEDGEMENTS
Thanks to Esme Choonara for cajoling and editing, and to
Weyman Bennett, Sally Campbell and Brian Richardson for reading
and helpful suggestions.
Also to Simon Basketter for fantastic picture research and
Simon Guy, Lina Nicolli and Mary Phillips for production assistance.

ABOUT THE AUTHOR
Yuri Prasad is a soul and jazz fanatic living in east London.

COVER IMAGE: 27 year old Martin Luther King photographed by
Alabama cops following his 1956 arrest during the Montgomery Bus
Boycott. The picture was rediscovered in 2004 by a deputy cleaning
out a Montgomery County Sheriff's Department storage room.
INSIDE FRONT: Marchers in Harlem, New York, carrying a banner
supporting civil rights protesters facing police violence in Selma,
Alabama, 1965.
INSIDE BACK: Striking sanitation workers assembling for a solidarity
march in Memphis, 28 March, 1968.

Published by Bookmarks Publications 2018
ISBN print edition: 978-1-910885-75-8
ISBN Kindle: 978-1-910885-76-5
ISBN ePub: 978-1-910885-77-2
ISBN PDF: 978-1-910885-78-9

Printed by Melita Press
Series design by noeldouglas.net

A Rebel's Guide to
MARTIN LUTHER
KING

YURI PRASAD

★ 1:
INTRODUCTION

There are few people today who openly criticise Martin Luther King and the struggle for civil rights that he helped lead. Indeed, King's life is celebrated by the establishment, both here and in the US. David Cameron, the former British prime minister who helped inject hatred of migrants into politics, declared in 2015, "[King] remains an inspiration to millions of people... Let his dream never die." Even US President Donald Trump agrees, testifying, apparently without any sense of irony, that King was "a man I have studied, watched, and admired for my entire life".

Such odious characters praise King today in part because they regard the issues he fought over as settled. Like the plantation slavery from which America derived its early wealth, the system of racial segregation that King opposed is now the stuff of history books, they insist. But King is also regarded as "safe" because his preaching of Christian forgiveness and the doctrine of non-violence is thought less threatening than the radical rhetoric and strategies that later came to dominate the movement for black liberation. But this caricature of a man, bold in language but "meek" in action, a liberal rebel, bears little resemblance to reality.

Where in the establishment's vision is the King who stood out against the Vietnam War in the period before that stance was acceptable in the mainstream? Where is the King who pledged to organise a poor people's march on

Washington, saying, "People ought to come to Washington, sit down if necessary in the middle of the street and say, 'We are here; we are poor; we don't have any money; you have made us this way...and we've come to stay until you do something about it'."? What about the King who mounted an ever more devastating critique of the system and talked of revolution, or the King that the government and the FBI labelled "the most dangerous Negro in America"? And where is the King that was gunned down at a Memphis motel while supporting refuse workers who were on strike in the city?

The answer is that the radical interpretation of Martin Luther King, especially the King that he came to be in the final years of his life, cannot be absorbed by the system easily, and as such must be rubbed out by reams of platitudes and ceremony—by sainthood. King did not come to the movement a fully-formed leader ready for action, in fact, in his early years in Montgomery he didn't even see himself as a leader at all. His experiences in the struggle helped develop his ideas and caused him to question and change his views on many subjects, not least on the economic and social system.

The establishment today takes for granted that the "Jim Crow" racial segregation that King opposed in the 1950s and 1960s was an aberration, something alien to modern capitalism. Certainly the laws which prevented inter-racial mixing, the crude signs demarking "coloured" and "white" areas, and the days of relentlessly regular lynching of black people are indeed gone—but the racism that King fought remains.

Today unarmed black men are seven times more likely than whites to die by police gunfire, African-American women earn less than 64 percent of the pay of white men, and there are more than a million African-Americans in prison, with black men being jailed at six times the rate of white men. This has been the context for the spectacular rise of the Black Lives Matter movement. The problem of racism and oppression is far from restricted to the US. It is a global problem facing billions of people, a problem that appears to thrive in the countries that first gave it life—the former colonial masters that have never accepted the loss of their empires.

Looking back at the early civil rights struggles, King admitted that he had conceived of the fight as being for reform of the system. He thought that, faced with the realities of black rebellion and racist resistance in the South, Washington could be persuaded to act to outlaw segregation, enshrine voting rights and create the conditions in which a true "brotherhood" could grow. His was, at that time, a patriotic vision—an endorsement of the American Dream even. But towards the end of his time, with the White House liberals silent as one black ghetto after another exploded in rage, it became clear to him that the oppression of black people in the US was hard-wired into the system. That realisation had major implications. If capitalism breeds what King believed to be the "nightmare" of "racism, poverty, militarism and materialism", what kind of system, and what kind of movement, are needed to replace it?

The answers were not entirely clear to King at the time of his assassination on 4 April, 1968, but the questions would continue to be central to the movement against racism that continued after his death. Indeed, they are the most important questions for everyone fighting racism today.

★ 2:
FROM
BOYCOTTS
TO
SIT-INS

In the wake of the Second World War millions of colonial subjects in Africa and Asia renewed their fight for freedom and were soon rewarded with a flood of victories. But black soldiers from the American Deep South returned from war not as conquering heroes who had beaten the menace of fascism, but as the second class citizens they were when they left. The democracy they fought for in Europe was denied to them at home. The laws and customs that segregated Southern society and enshrined white rule were largely intact. The land that was once tilled by black slaves was still tended by the black poor. Jim Crow was made up of state and local laws that enforced racial segregation in the former Confederate states of the US Civil War. They mandated that all public facilities be divided for blacks and whites, with black people invariably receiving worse treatment and limited services. Schools, colleges, and many workplaces across the South were subject to Jim Crow. Officially sanctioned segregation in the armed forces didn't end until 1948.

Yet beneath the surface there were changes, and soon they would coalesce into the beginnings of a movement. As the demand for factory labour grew in the war years and during the post-war boom, many black families abandoned farming and sharecropping and headed to the cities, mainly in the North. Away from the plantations, in the factories and workshops, many found not only a collective voice but also a new anger. Here it wasn't the law that stopped them eating in a restaurant; it was lack of money.

The black middle classes also grew, chaffing at the restrictions placed upon them because of their colour. Why, given their status and wealth, were they denied the respect that they were entitled to, they asked. The two trends taken together gave rise to what some termed the "New Negro". Their growing frustration was behind a series of legal challenges by black organisations in the mid-1950s which ultimately led the Supreme Court to overrule the Southern states and declare racially segregated education illegal. Many now asked, if racism could be outlawed in education, could the same method be applied across the board?

But the Southern establishment was not going to give in without a fight. It declared that it would put up "Massive Resistance", both legal and illegal, to the federal instructions. The pace of change, despite a string of legal victories, was agonisingly slow. If segregation were to be overturned there would have to be action not only in the courtroom but on the streets. The changing class character of black people fed into a new spirit, meaning such action was not far off.

In December 1955 the arrest of Rosa Parks for refusing to give up her bus seat to a white passenger sparked a year-long boycott that began the Civil Rights Movement in earnest. Parks is often presented as a

simple seamstress, tired and frustrated—someone who
acted spontaneously, rather than out of commitment.
In fact, she was a long-standing activist who had spent
time in the company of Communists during the 1930s and
more recently with left radicals at the Highlander Folk
School. She said of herself, "I had almost a life history of
being rebellious about being mistreated because of my
colour." (Jack M. Bloom, *Class, Race and the Civil Rights
Movement*, Indiana University Press, 1987, p132)

Jo Ann Robinson of the Montgomery Women's
Political Council immediately took up Park's case, over-
night producing 52,500 leaflets calling for a bus boycott,
and spreading the word through Montgomery's churches.

But it was a 26 year old, newly-arrived, preacher
called Martin Luther King who shot to prominence as
the leader of the 40,000-strong movement. The Atlanta-
born reverend was only recently out of college where
he had studied divinity and was now the pastor of the
city's Dexter Avenue Baptist Church. A charismatic and
much sought after sermoniser, the young minister was
radical but liberal. Under the influence of his teachers, he
embraced the philosophy of civil disobedience theorised
by Henry David Thoreau and practised by Gandhi in the
movement for Indian independence. He saw the coming
struggle for black rights as one for the right to integrate
fully into American society, the right not to be cast as
"separate but equal", as the Southern law books invariably declared. Despite the Cold War witch-hunts, King
also wanted to understand the appeal of socialism, writing that communism "should challenge every Christian—as
it challenged me—to a growing concern about social justice. With all of its false assumption and evil methods

communism grew as a protest against the hardships of the underprivileged." (Cornell West, ed, *The Radical King*, Beacon Press, 2015, p42)

Coretta Scott King, Martin's wife, will doubtless also have been an influence on him. She was already a civil rights activist before she met her husband and had been a member of the left wing Progressive Party in the 1940s. A talented classical singer, she once held ambitions to a professional career but in 1950s America women were allowed few options other than marrying and staying at home to raise a family. But giving up her on her goals was not the only sacrifice she would make. Long before the time of the boycott Coretta's life was one surrounded by threats of violence. As a child she witnessed her white neighbours burn down her family's lumber mill. In the course of the Civil Rights Movement she was repeatedly threatened and abused, shot at, and saw her own house bombed.

As the boycott in Montgomery gained pace King became ever more prominent. He appeared on the front cover of *Time* magazine and held a phone conversation with the US president. He responded to attacks that sought to paint him as a Communist by emphasising his commitment to non-violence and brotherhood, while downplaying his earlier anti-capitalist inclinations.

Throughout 1956 some 95 percent of black people in Montgomery refused to use the buses, while nearly a hundred campaigners, including King, were arrested. Millions of Americans watched the drama unfold nightly on their TVs, but beyond them the world watched eagerly as the "great democracy" floundered. As the pressure on the establishment grew, the Supreme Court moved to outlaw segregation on Montgomery buses.

The victory sent a shockwave through the South. Desperate to hammer home his advantage, King urged others to follow Montgomery, and reached out to scores of young ministers in towns across the South, thereby creating a new, radical leadership that was to become an organisation called the Southern Christian Leadership Conference (SCLC). Soon the mood of resistance spread to bus boycotts in Florida, and Birmingham, and from there to Little Rock, Arkansas, where in 1957 nine black students were blocked from integrating into the Central High School.

The SCLC leaders were learning in struggle and their ideas underwent rapid change. After Montgomery, King wrote:

"Feeling that our demands were moderate, I had assumed they would be granted, I had assumed that they would be granted with little question: I had believed that the privileged would give up their privileges on request. This experience, however, taught me a lesson. I came to see that no one gives up his privileges without strong resistance. I saw further that the underlying purpose of segregation was to oppress and exploit the segregated, not simply to keep them apart." (Bloom, p140)

Churches were to play a central role in the movement over the next decade. Pastors, who were employed by their congregations, could act with a degree of independence that few other black people could match. Their churches were seen as a place of relative safety—where a large group of black people could gather legitimately. The biblical parables that spoke of long-suffering people ultimately being rewarded by god chimed with many who knew well the penalties for resisting.

Christian doctrines that praised those who "turned the other cheek" when struck by an oppressor fed the non-violent strategy that dominated the movement. As a largely poor and generally unarmed minority, this approach appealed to many black people. Southern black people in particular felt the odds were stacked against them if the battle for equal rights came down to a gun fight. Many accepted the tactical need to be non-violent, even if they didn't necessarily accept the principle. King's stress on civil disobedience also worked as a means of broadening the movement, allowing maximum numbers to participate.

King's strategy had another effect—it reassured liberal middle class whites and moderate well-to-do blacks that they had nothing to fear from his movement. They could press Washington to bring forward more reforms without risking violent confrontation.

But this method carried a contradiction at its heart. While the movement was only rarely violent in response to the aggression it faced, its participants demanded that Washington uphold Supreme Court judgements by over-ruling state authorities. At Little Rock, and countless other confrontations in the years ahead, that meant the threat of armed troops under federal orders forcibly impos-ing change on Southern police and state troopers, white citizen councils and the Ku Klux Klan. King's non-violent strategy ultimately rested on Washington's guns.

But for now, these debates were a side issue. The newly founded movement was discovering its strength and spreading its influence.

★ 3: STUDENTS AND GROWING RADICALISM

At 4.30pm on Monday 1 February 1960 four black students from a local college sat down at the lunch counter of Woolworths in Greenboro, North Carolina. They knew well that the café was segregated and that they were sitting in a "whites only" area. The waiting staff would not serve them, but rather than move or leave, the students stayed seated until closing time. The next day they returned, but with 16 new recruits. Despite heckles and threats from white customers, the students refused to move and instead read their books. Now the newspapers and TV were interested. On the third day 60 students came to Woolworths. On the fourth 300 people took part, so many that the "sit-in" as it became known had to spread to other segregated stores nearby. Within three months the movement had spread to 50 cities in 13 states, and some 50,000 students were involved.

It was inevitable that the spirit gripping the South would spread to college campuses. The new recruits, mostly in their teens and very early twenties, would take no lessons on "being patient" and demanded change now. They respected and were inspired by King, but at 31 years old to some he seemed part of the old guard. They needed organisation and created the Student Non-violent Coordinating

Committee (SNCC). Whereas half a decade earlier the young reverends had been the radical cutting edge of the movement, now it was SNCC that would set the pace. Their dynamism and numbers pulled the whole Civil Rights Movement, young and old, into a more radical phase. Campaigners threw their energy into the Freedom Rides, in which inter-racial groups of coach passengers deliberately provoked local states that maintained segregated facilities. Southern mobs attacked coaches, setting them on fire, and the riders were often badly beaten, yet the Rides continued. Brave volunteers ventured deep into Ku Klux Klan territory to mount voter registration drives to gain black Southerners basic democratic rights, and many paid dearly for their efforts [see page 12].

King greeted the arrival of new forces enthusiastically and was himself arrested and sentenced to four months hard labour after a sit-in at a department store in his home town of Atlanta. But now he often found himself straddling the movement's divergent wings. On one side stood influential white liberals, and older, more conservative black organisations, which described themselves as "friends" but worried that the new radicalism would lead to rebellion. They demanded King calm things down. On the other side stood the new, younger forces that viewed the conservatives as an obstacle every bit as menacing as Jim Crow. King was trying to use the anger at the slow pace of change as a means of pressurising the new Kennedy administration to get off the fence and back new civil rights legislation but seeking an alliance with Washington risked alienating the youth who began referring to him as "De Lawd".

By 1963 King's SCLC were desperate for a victory in order to maintain the alliance, and they needed it to be big.

FANNIE LOU HAMER

*Leading activist who helped register 63,000 black people
from Mississippi into the Freedom Democratic Party,
which opposed the racism of the Southern Democrats.*

❝ I reckon the most horrible experience I've had
was in June of 1963. I was arrested along with
several others in Winona, Mississippi. That's in
Montgomery County, the county where I was born.
I was carried to a cell and locked up with Euvester
Simpson. I began to hear the sound of licks, and I
could hear people screaming...

After then, the State Highway patrolmen came
and carried me out of the cell into another cell
where there were two Negro prisoners. The patrolman gave the first Negro a long blackjack [baton] that
was heavy. It was loaded with something and they
had me lay down on the bunk with my face down,
and I was beat. I was beat by the first Negro till he
gave out. Then the patrolman ordered the other man
to take the blackjack and he began to beat...

After I got out of jail, half dead, I found out that
Medgar Evers had been shot down in his own yard."
(Clayborne Carson et al, eds, *The Eyes on the Prize
Civil Rights Reader*, Penguin, 1991, p177)

★ 4: BALLAD OF BIRMINGHAM

King and the leadership set their sights on Birmingham, Alabama—for many the citadel of the racist South. The city was 40 percent black— yet it had not a single black firefighter, bus driver, bank clerk, police officer or shop cashier. When the US federal government demanded that parks be desegregated in 1961, the city government responded by closing all public parks. King explained, "We believed that while a campaign in Birmingham would surely be the toughest fight of our civil rights careers, it could, if successful, break the back of segregation all over the nation... A victory there might well set forces in motion to change the entire course of the drive for freedom and justice." (Bloom, p174)

Campaigners wanted to target the city's commerce, to launch so many sit-ins and marches simultaneously that business would grind to a halt, the jails would overflow and the state would give in to the pressure. They hoped to split the city's business class, many of whom were ambivalent about segregation, from the political class who were absolutely dependent on it. To do so meant bringing in activists from outside to the city, but most importantly, appealing to black working class people from Birmingham to come out in their thousands—something of a departure for the movement. Battle commenced on 3 April 1963 with a series of marches but not on the scale needed. King and the other leaders mounted daily calls for more support.

Manning Marable records the effect of King's appeal at a massive church rally where he castigated black preachers who had ignored the demonstrations. King said, "I'm tired of preachers riding around in big cars, living in fine homes, but not willing to take their part in the fight. If you can't stand up with your people, you are not fit to be a leader... We are winning the struggle for which we have sacrificed, but we must even be ready to die to be free, if that is what's necessary." (Manning Marable, *Race, Reform and Rebellion*, University Press of Mississippi, 1990, p70)

When Ralph Abernathy, King's deputy in the movement, rose to his feet, he asked the congregation who would volunteer to go to jail with him and Martin. "Men, women and children surged forward, hands upraised, tears in their eyes, singing and praying." (Marable, p70)

King and Abernathy were arrested on Good Friday but even that was not enough to force change, so Martin called on school pupils to join the protests.

In front of TV cameras from across the world Birmingham police let loose everything they had at the children who were kneeling in the street to pray. The police set vicious police dogs on the young people and attacked them with powerful fire hoses. Birmingham's jails were filled to capacity by mass arrests. Inside the cells many were bleeding and had suffered broken bones, but defiance remained intact. In the days that followed, the children return to the streets again and again.

In the midst of the battle, a group of moderate white ministers from the city denounced King, insisting he should show more patience and fight the battle against segregation exclusively in the courts. King replied with one of the most famous essays in US history, Letter from a Birmingham Jail [see page 16].

With righteous indignation, he took on those who opposed the protests, writing, "...over the last few years I have been gravely disappointed with the white moderate. I have almost reached the regrettable conclusion that the Negroes' great stumbling block in the stride toward freedom is not the White Citizens' 'Councillor' or the Ku Klux Klanner, but the white moderate who is more devoted to 'order' than to justice." (Carson, p157)

Revulsion at the police's racist brutality spread across America and across the world. The US, engaged in the height of the Cold War and desperate to bring countries emerging from colonialism into its sphere, was embarrassed by these scenes of violence on home soil. By the middle of May, after several weeks of beatings and arrests, President Kennedy was finally forced to act. Behind the scenes he pressurised city business leaders and authorities into a plan to desegregate public facilities. Not long after, his administration announced a new civil rights bill that would outlaw segregation throughout the nation. It was a massive victory for the movement, and for King.

KING'S LETTER FROM A BIRMINGHAM JAIL

" We have waited for more than 340 years for our constitutional and God given rights. The nations of Asia and Africa are moving with jet-like speed toward gaining political independence, but we still creep at horse and buggy pace toward gaining a cup of coffee at a lunch counter. Perhaps it is easy for those who have never felt the stinging darts of segregation to say, 'Wait.'

But when you have seen vicious mobs lynch your mothers and fathers at will and drown your sisters and brothers at whim; when you have seen hate filled policemen curse, kick and even kill your black brothers and sisters; when you see the vast majority of your twenty million Negro brothers smothering in an airtight cage of poverty in the midst of an affluent society; when you suddenly find your tongue twisted and your speech stammering as you seek to explain to your six year old daughter why she can't go to the public amusement park that has just been advertised on television, and see tears welling up in her eyes when she is told that Funtown is closed to colored children, and see ominous clouds of inferiority beginning to form in her little mental sky, and see her beginning to distort her personality by developing an unconscious bitterness toward white people; when you

have to concoct an answer for a five year old son who is asking: 'Daddy, why do white people treat colored people so mean?'; when you take a cross county drive and find it necessary to sleep night after night in the uncomfortable corners of your automobile because no motel will accept you; when you are humiliated day in and day out by nagging signs reading 'white' and 'colored'; when your first name becomes 'nigger', your middle name becomes 'boy' (however old you are) and your last name becomes 'John', and your wife and mother are never given the respected title 'Mrs'; when you are harried by day and haunted by night by the fact that you are a Negro, living constantly at tip-toe stance, never quite knowing what to expect next, and are plagued with inner fears and outer resentments; when you are forever fighting a degenerating sense of 'nobodiness'—then you will understand why we find it difficult to wait.

There comes a time when the cup of endurance runs over, and men are no longer willing to be plunged into the abyss of despair. I hope, sirs, you can understand our legitimate and unavoidable impatience."

★ 5: MARCHING ON WASHINGTON

The year 1963 marked a turning point in the battle for civil rights. A mood of angry impatience gripped the tens of thousands of overwhelmingly young activists that now swelled the movement's ranks. In the period between June and the March on Washington in August there were some 758 demonstrations in 186 cities, resulting in 14,733 arrests. The demand for "Freedom Now" was more than just a slogan—it was the defiant chant of those who rejected talk of "slow change". King was to capture the feeling in the title of his book, Why We Can't Wait, in which he described the Civil Rights Movement as America's "Negro Revolution". Images of protesters in the streets of Birmingham still filled the media and, as months passed, these were supplanted with pictures of burning buildings during bombings and the riots that followed. It was easy to believe that King had called it right when he talked of revolution.

Many activists saw the March on Washington as a chance to shut down the capital with sit-ins at railway stations, on the highways and at the airport. They wanted to stay until the South's racist laws were overturned.

The march came 100 years after the Emancipation Proclamation during the Civil War that formally ended slavery. It would turn the spotlight on the white liberals in government who said they opposed segregation, but who would do nothing to outlaw it. Many were distrustful of Kennedy's administration. He faced pressure from the movement, both its moderate and radical wings, but he also relied heavily on the Democratic Party machine in the South, known as the Dixiecrats. The Southern party machine was determined that no new anti-segregation laws should come forward and Kennedy worried that if he pressed them too hard they would split from the party and go over to the Republicans. Those twin pressures meant that Washington seemed, at best, an unreliable ally. Kennedy had only recently declared this was "not the right time" for civil rights legislation but then, after Birmingham, had announced new legislation, knowing this was the only way to head off further confrontation.

"The events in Birmingham and elsewhere have so increased the cries for equality that no city or state or legislative body can prudently choose to ignore them," declared the president, in a hastily-convened broadcast. But Kennedy, and the Democratic Party machine that surrounded him, also made demands of the movement. The price of legislation was that the coming March on Washington be transformed into a celebratory endorsement of the government. Moderates were expected to control radicals, and King, as a figure who tried to hold both wings together, was expected to play a pivotal role.

The prize of the first federal anti-segregation laws since the Civil War was too big for King to resist.

Nevertheless, the state shuddered at the thought of thousands of black people marching through the capital and was "fully prepared for the anticipated disorder, even insurrection: Washington virtually under martial law; five surrounding military bases on full alert; 19,000 heavily

JOYCE LADNER

Civil rights campaign worker

"We went to Washington the day before the march. Malcolm X held forth in the Hilton hotel lobby all afternoon. I was absolutely mesmerised by him. So were a lot of others because there was a crowd of people around him all the time. I remember that he called the March on Washington, the 'Farce on Washington'. It gave me a lot to think about. Were we engaged in a farce? Had I spent the summer working on a cause that was nothing more than a show? I decided not.

I also remember the big flag about John's speech. [He said] that if the violence did not stop, we would have no choice but to march through the South the way that General Sherman did, burning everything in its wake.

[We] were quite angry about the demand that the speech be changed. What I remember most is standing on the podium looking out at the 250,000 people. I felt emboldened because of the large number who came. I didn't feel so isolated anymore."

(Joyce Ladner, *The March on Washington*, crmvet. org/info/mowjoyce.htm) armed special forces ready to be airlifted in thirty large helicopters; several hundred inmates freed from D.C. jails to make room for protesters; and among hundreds of FBI agents circulating in the crowd, one planted just offstage at the Lincoln Memorial ready to pull the plug on any incendiary rhetoric, to be replaced by a vinyl recording of Mahalia Jackson singing a spiritual." (Stewart Burns, *We Will Stand Here Till We Die*, Amazon, 2013, loc 1226)

The text of every speech was to be previewed by Kennedy's staff and a selection of moderate black leaders. John Lewis, of the Student Non-violent Co-ordinating Committee (SNCC), wanted to say Kennedy's entrance into the battle for civil rights was "too little, too late". But his speech was censored. Nevertheless, Lewis, who much later became a leading Democratic Party politician, got huge applause when he spoke from the podium, saying, "We will splinter the segregated South into a thousand pieces and put them back together in the image of God and democracy... We cannot stop, and we will not be patient." (Burns, loc 1260)

Whatever misgivings grassroots activists may have had about the way the protest had been taken over were muted by the sheer numbers that came to join it. Between a quarter and a third of a million arrived in Washington on Wednesday 28 August, 1963. It was the biggest march in the history of the capital, dwarfing the previous record holder—the Ku Klux Klan in 1925! There were 22 chartered trains, 2,000 charted buses, and thousands of car pools. And, some marchers endured a more dangerous journey. Robert Avery and a group of friends hitched from Alabama. Despite segregation, almost all those who picked up the three black teens were white. As the group drove through the mountains of Tennessee they saw effigies of black people hanging outside service stations.

"The dummies they hung out, the Rebel flags hanging from lampposts," Robert recalls, "that was sending a strong message... People understood that you can't stop here." (Michelle Norris, Determined To Reach 1963 March, Teen Used Thumb And Feet, npr.org/2013/08/14/210470828/determined-to-reach-1963-march-teen-used-thumb-and-feet)

The march was estimated at about three-quarters black, one-quarter white and Latino, and contained a large contingent of organised labour—despite the main national union federation refusing to back it. The numbers mattered. The hundreds of thousands in the streets filled people with a sense of their own power. No longer could it be said that civil rights were the concern of only a minority. The march, rather than announcing the conclusion of the struggle for civil rights, instead opened up another new phase, with ever more radical demands and tactics coming to the fore.

Martin Luther King's "I have a Dream" speech, which he delivered on the day, is rightly commemorated as one of the greatest of all time. The mainstream media always focus on its depiction of a future where children enjoy life without racial barriers, but it also contained passages far less palatable to the powerful—ones that continue to resonate. He said that 100 years after the Emancipation Proclamation, "the Negro is still sadly crippled by the manacles of segregation and the chains of discrimination. One hundred years later, the Negro lives on a lonely island of poverty in the midst of a vast ocean of material prosperity. One hundred years later, the Negro is still languishing in the corners of the American society and finds himself in exile in his own land."

★ 6: BACKLASH BLUES

If Kennedy and the Democrats had hoped that a peaceful march would help relieve pressure from the movement they were mistaken. Less than a month after the protest, "Dynamite Bob" Chambliss told his family in Alabama that he'd found the address of "the nigger girl that was going to integrate the school". He boasted that he had "enough stuff put away to flatten half of Birmingham".

On Sunday 15 September 1963, at 10.22 am, a deafening bang could be heard all over the city. A bomb outside the Sixteenth Street Baptist Church had blasted a seven-foot wide hole through a thick wall behind which was a Sunday school class. Addie Mae Collins, 14, was tying the sash of her friend Denise McNair, 11. Carole Robertson and Cynthia Wesley, both 14, were doing their hair. After the smoke cleared, and the heavy rubble lifted away, four charred bodies were found. One was decapitated, and their identities could only be established through their shoes and jewellery. More than 20 other church-goers were injured in the blast.

For the rest of the day, black people sought revenge and battled the police that so brutalised them. A white teenager shot dead a 13 year old black boy riding a bicycle and cops killed a black man trying to escape the fighting. Black men patrolled their neighbourhoods armed with shotguns. Few who were in Birmingham that week believed the non-violence that had characterised the Civil Rights Movement was appropriate now—even reverends joined the self-defence groups. The bombing was a sign of what the segregationists now meant when they talked of "Massive Resistance". Black people supposedly had Washington and its laws on their side, but when it came down to it, neither were to be seen.

★ 7: THE CRISIS YEARS

Whatever clouds were on the horizon, King was riding high. Following the success of the Birmingham campaign, the March on Washington, and the subsequent signing of the Civil Rights Act into law in July 1964, he was catapulted into being a global figure, someone millions of people, black and white, regarded as their leader. The new law outlawed many of the practices that stopped black people from being able to register to vote, and prohibited racial segregation in schools, employment and public services. *Time* magazine named King 1963's "Person of the Year" and he was awarded the Nobel Peace Prize the following year. All around the world people pored over his books and speeches, and many tried to apply his theories of civil disobedience to their own campaigns. In something less than a decade King's movement had changed America forever.

In his London Nobel Prize acceptance speech, King said:

"I'm still convinced that nonviolence is the most potent weapon available to oppressed people in their struggle for freedom and justice. It has a way of disarming the opponent, exposing his moral defences. It weakens his morale, and at the same time it works on his conscience, and he just doesn't know how to handle it. If he doesn't beat you, wonderful. If he beats you, you develop the quiet courage of accepting blows without retaliating. If he doesn't put you in jail, wonderful. Nobody with any sense loves to go to jail. But if he puts you in jail, you go in that jail and transform it from a dungeon of shame to a haven of freedom and human dignity... if a man has not discovered something that he will die for, he isn't fit to live." (King, 1964, democracynow.org/2015/1/19/exclusive_newly_discovered_1964_mlk_speech)

The message was popular globally, but among civil rights activists the mood was much darker. Southern resistance to the tide of desegregation may have been futile, but it was real—and the shorter its remaining time, the more vicious it became. White authorities in many towns and cities gleefully refused federal orders to desegregate, and white gangs backed by cops unleashed terror upon black people and those who fought for civil rights. During the Freedom Summer of 1964 over a thousand activists were arrested, 80 were beaten, 37 churches were bombed or burnt, four civil rights workers were killed, four were critically wounded and at least three black people from Mississippi were murdered because of their support for the movement. Many activists started to ask where the white liberals were when they were needed, and to question whether non-violence was always a useful tactic. Some SNCC activists now advocated carrying guns when campaigning in parts of the South.

The coalition which had fought segregation was also by now wracked by division over the place of white people in the struggle. The government's slow pace of change and urging of "patience" fed growing cynicism about whites in general, with many SNCC activists now believing that only black people could genuinely fight racism. The widely accepted notion that the Civil Rights Movement stood for integration faced scrutiny. When King talked about "brotherhood" he meant more than legalistic equality between blacks and whites—he pointed towards a more fundamental equality in which all races would live in harmony. The trouble was that many in the movement no longer believed that was possible, and there were some who had come to the conclusion that it was not even desirable.

As far as the establishment was concerned, the battle against segregation was now reaching a conclusion, with the coming Voting Rights Act being the last piece of legislation they were prepared to offer. Former Vice President Lyndon Baines Johnson replaced Kennedy after his assassination in November 1963 and King was quick to both endorse him and argue that the movement should give him time and space before putting further demands on his administration. With some justification, King believed that his strategy of creating pressure on Washington had won crucial changes. Certainly, in narrow terms, and with a deal of hindsight, that was true. Within five years of the Voting Rights Act being passed the percentage of black adults registered to vote in the South rose dramatically, with Alabama growing from 19.3 to 61.3 percent and Mississippi rising from 6.7 percent to 60.4 percent. But, asked the radicals, what use was the vote if the parties elected to Washington merely acted to continue the racism of the system? What was the point of fighting for integration if that meant accepting many of the inequalities of US society?

Under pressure, King knew he needed another victory, and that somehow he had to pull the civil rights coalition back together for one more fight. But what then happened in Selma was only to deepen the fracture lines in his movement.

Campaigning in Selma, Alabama, began with the SNCC in 1963 with the aim of outlawing literacy tests and other barriers put up to stop black people from registering to vote. Yet despite much effort and the building of a solid local base, the campaign suffered as the authorities cracked down with brutality. In 1965, after the murder of a civil rights activist by a state trooper, the SCLC decided to organise a march from Selma to the state capital of Montgomery some 50 miles away. The hope was that, just as in Birmingham two years previously, the sight of racist police brutality would sicken the nation and Washington would be forced to act.

In all three marches made to leave Selma across the Edmund Pettus Bridge. As the first crossed the country line, state troopers and a mob of white racists attacked the approximately two thousand marchers with billy clubs and tear gas, leaving many badly injured. Amelia Boynton was clubbed and overcome by the gas. She recalls, "The police department came up and started beating us, and I stood up there, then finally I fell... I fell when the posse or whoever it was hit me, and it was below my shoulder, and I looked at him like I thought he was crazy, and he said, 'Run.' Then he hit the back of my neck, and I was unconscious." (CBS, Voices of the Selma march, 50 years ago, cbsnews.com/news/selma-bloody-sunday-civil-rights-march-50th-anniversary/)

Marcher and SNCC activist John Lewis was also hospitalised. He recalls saying, "I don't know how President Johnson can send troops to Vietnam... but he can't send troops to protect people in this country who only want to register and vote." (Nick Kotz, *Judgment Days: Lyndon Baines Johnson, Martin Luther King Jr., and the Laws That Changed America*, Marnier, 2006, p285)

Absent for the first, King rallied his troops for a second march two days later having made a secret deal with LBJ's advisers that they would not confront the police. In return Washington agreed to advance the Voting Rights Bill giving King the much need victory. LBJ even made a televised address to the nation, where he repeatedly used the phrase, "We shall overcome." As protesters on the second march reached the police lines, the cops parted as if to let the marchers through, but King then instructed his followers to about turn and march back into Selma. King said he feared a trap, and maybe one was planned, but his actions sent waves of fury among the younger activists. The third march was 25,000-strong and took place later in the month. On LBJ's command, it was now sheltered by 1,900 members of the Alabama National Guard under federal command.

Historian and activist Vincent Harding expressed the bitterness about the Selma that many felt:

"When the time came to assert their right to march for freedom, there is every evidence that King backed off. Listening to the mediators from President Johnson, he refused to press the movement into so harsh and predictably bloody a confrontation. Many sagging spirits were finally broken with that act of retreat, and the distrust that had been building against King, SCLC and the Johnson administration poured out in deep anger and disgust." (Marable, p80)

★ 8: GHETTOS, RIOTS AND REBELLION

In 1963 the black radical writer James Baldwin predicted that race riots would soon "spread to every metropolitan centre in the nation which has a significant Negro population... It is because the nation, the entire nation, has spent a hundred years avoiding the question of the place of the black man in it." (James Baldwin, Nobody Knows My Name, Penguin, 1991) He was right.

Between 1964 and 1968 black people rose up in almost every city in the north east, the Midwest and California. When the Watts district of Los Angeles exploded in rage in 1965, the authorities deployed 15,000 armed police and National Guards. In the repression that followed 34 people died and 4,000 were arrested. Even Watts would later be dwarfed. In most cases the trigger for the explosion was confrontation with racist, and overwhelmingly white, police officers. But behind the everyday harassment stood poverty, unemployment, ghetto housing and poor education—second class citizenship in all but name.

King's attitude to the social unrest was contradictory. He was keen to empathise with ghetto inhabitants, famously describing riots as "the language of the unheard". However, mindful of Washington and his liberal backers, he also co-signed an open letter that called riots "criminal acts" and called for them to be dealt with as such.

Many younger activists went further than sympathising with the causes, and instead saw the riots as an admissible expression of rage. Far from "criminal", these were uprisings, insurrections even, which had something in common with the freedom struggles being waged around the world. From Malcolm X, the black nationalist, and Franz Fanon, the revolutionary anti-colonialist, they learned that violence of the oppressed was a just response to the violence of the conditions that millions of poor black people endured. The urban risings were also a confirmation that racism could no longer be considered a "Southern problem".

The urban rebellions had another effect—they declared that black people in the poorest parts of the cities were not to be considered merely victims; they were people who could fight back. The density of the cities, the concentration of sections of the population into ghettos, and the absence of a middle class there to act as a buffer, were for some a potential source of unity and power. Rather than simply spontaneous, unplanned actions committed by "criminals", the rioters were themselves political, often leaving black-owned businesses alone, and torching the shops where they had been abused, or where the shop keepers refused black people credit. For many involved, the riots were a source of pride, not shame.

This form of community resistance found a ready form of expression in the term "Black Power!" The phrase, which had originated with SNCC leader Stokely Carmichael in 1966, spread like wildfire through both the Civil Rights Movement and the ghettos. Its definition may have been imprecise, and the politics of those who used it varied enormously, yet its grip was undeniable. King knew that the situation in the North threatened to make him and his non-violent strategy irrelevant. Touring Watts during the last day of the riot he was confronted by a young man who declared, "We won!" Pointing to the smoke and destruction around him, King asked how he could say that. "Because we made them pay attention to us," the man responded.

Somehow the SCLC needed to prove that its winning tactics from the South could be applied in the riot-torn cities. Its leadership chose Chicago to be the site of an experimental first campaign in the North targeting housing, jobs and education. In 1966 the SCLC led a coalition of groups which demanded city authorities not only change laws, but also initiate a major redistribution of wealth—a demand far more radical than any levelled in the Southern campaigns.

At its height, the Chicago campaign put several thousand on the streets but failed to create the kind of crisis that had on several occasions forced Washington to intervene. The city authorities simply refused to budge and the strength of the white opposition took everybody by surprise. During one march King was felled by a rock thrown by a racist, and had to be led away. Perhaps more damaging was the way white liberals in the media and in office castigated him for daring to tell them how to conduct their affairs. It soon became clear that the Northern Democrats who had played such a crucial role as part of the alliance against segregation would not support him against their friends in the city.

The ultimate failure of the Chicago plan was masked by a series of agreements with city authorities, agreements that were quickly reneged upon. The effect of the failure did more than demoralise King and his supporters; it boosted those who pioneered a more radical approach, something that King was to acknowledge:

"In all the speaking that I have done in the United States before varied audiences, including some hostile whites, the only time that I have been booed was one night in a Chicago mass meeting by some young members of the Black Power movement. I went home that night with an ugly feeling. Selfishly I thought of my sufferings and sacrifices over the last twelve years. Why would they boo one so close to them? But as I lay awake thinking, I finally came to myself, and I could not for the life of me have less than patience and understanding for those young people. For twelve years I, and others like me, had held out radiant promises of progress. I had preached to them about my dream. I had lectured to them about the not too distant day when they would have freedom, 'all, here and now.' I had urged them to have faith in America and in white society. Their hopes had soared. They were now booing because they felt that we were unable to deliver on our promises. They were booing because we had urged them to have faith in people who had too often proved to be unfaithful. They were now hostile because they were watching the dream that they had so readily accepted turn into a frustrating nightmare." (Martin Luther King, *Where do we go from here: chaos or community?*, Beacon Press, 1968, p49)

★ 9: MARTIN AND MALCOLM

While King was angered and perturbed by the Black Power slogan, Malcolm X would not have been. The former leader of the Black Muslim group, the Nation of Islam, had for years urged younger activists in the Civil Rights Movement to break from King's "conciliatory" politics. He ridiculed King's integrationist strategies by pointing to the violence and hypocrisy of "white society", and he chastised those who advocated non-violence, insisting violence was both morally justified, and the only thing that the oppressor understood. In his time in the Nation he regularly called for black people to separate themselves from whites and build a new society for themselves.

While Malcolm's ideas carried relatively little weight in the South during the civil rights period, he had a following

of tens of thousands in the North—among the middle classes that cherished his ideal of a black society in which they would be boss, but also among the poorest, where his message of race pride and self-reliance fitted well with those who lacked means but lacked nothing in confidence.

But even in his Northern base Malcolm had a key weakness—the Nation of Islam's strict ban on members from engaging in politics or from any kind of social action, even in defence of the religion and its adherents. That made it easy for Malcolm's opponents to characterise him as someone who "talks big, but acts little". The criticism stung and Malcolm found himself straining against the limitations, ultimately breaking from the Nation and converting to Sunni Islam in 1964.

For the last year of his life Malcolm was free to go and say what he liked. Touring Africa, Europe and the Middle East his ideas entered a period of rapid change. He briefly met King that year and declared that now he too wanted to build a movement to challenge racism. His concept was more radical than King's at this time, and was largely focused on the black poor in the North. But from its inception it was hampered by a lack of forces to make it a reality. No longer describing whites as "devils", Malcolm was under the influence of the anti-colonial movements he had met on his travels. He now described the fight for a society free of racism as a "revolution", one in which whites who were "really fed up" had a place. In 1965, in one of Malcolm's last speeches before being killed by an assassin's bullet, he said:

"I believe that there will ultimately be a clash between the oppressed and those that do the oppressing. I believe that there will be a clash between those who want freedom, justice, and equality for everyone and those who want to continue the systems of exploitation... It is incorrect to classify the revolt of the Negro as simply a racial conflict of black against white, or as a purely American problem. Rather, we are today seeing a global rebellion of the oppressed against the oppressor, the exploited against the exploiter." (Marable, p86)

Malcolm and Martin seldom communicated, and even when they did, not always on friendly terms, but their visions of struggle were ultimately to coincide in ways that neither could foresee. Just a few years after Malcolm's speech, King would talk in similar terms, saying:

"These are revolutionary times. All over the globe men are revolting against old systems of exploitation and oppression, and out of the wombs of a frail world new systems of justice and equality are being born. The shirtless and barefoot people of the earth are rising up as never before. 'The people who sat in darkness have seen a great light.' We in the West must support these revolutions... Communism is a judgement on our failure to make democracy real and to follow through on the revolutions that we initiated." (King, 1968, p200)

It is commonplace for commentators to describe Malcolm and Martin as polar opposites, one radical and the other liberal; one for violence and one against; one for integration and one against. This simple dichotomy dominates even much left wing thinking but misses a great deal. Both were on a political journey at the time their lives were cut short, both were looking forward to a future in which racism was transcended, both were to conclude that it was impossible to get rid of racism without getting rid of capitalism, and both had concluded that if there was going to be a revolution, it would be the poor that made it.

★ 10: BLACK POWER TO POOR POWER

King took the argument about Black Power very seriously and rightly understood that its popularity marked an end point for the movement he had led. He spent long hours in discussion with those that advocated the slogan and readily conceded the need for black people to have real power. He read the books they cited, and he tested the arguments in his own mind by trying to see things from his opponents' position. The conclusion he reached was that the slogan had some "positives" but was "unfortunate" and sent "wrong signals" to adversaries and potential allies alike. It lacked any programme, and had no specific meaning, he charged. "The words 'black' and 'power' together give the impression that we are talking about black domination rather than black equality," he wrote. (King, 1968, p32)

But he was equally adamant that racism and the failure of white liberalism lay behind the slogan's growing success. "[Black Power] was born from the wounds of despair and disappointment. It is a cry of daily hurt and persistent pain. For centuries the Negro has been caught in the tentacles of white power. Many Negroes have given up faith in the white majority because 'white power' with total control has left them empty-handed." (King, 1968, p33)

In reality, Black Power gave expression to a generalised feeling that black liberation could no longer be considered contingent on whites, particularly those in positions of authority. No matter how reasoned King's argument, the new terrain of struggle meant that all those seeking radical means to take on racism gravitated towards the slogan—and in that sense it represented a clear advance for the movement. The trouble was, pretty soon right wing opponents of the movement had grasped the slogan's ambiguities and were themselves seeking to mobilise behind it. So future president, Richard Nixon, could write:

"Black extremists are guaranteed headlines when they shout 'burn' or 'get a gun,' but much of the black militant talk these days is actually in terms far closer to the doctrines of free enterprise than to those of the welfarist '30s." Nixon promised "more black ownership, black pride, black jobs, black opportunity, and yes, black power". (Marable, 1991, p98)

The process of dissecting Black Power also forced King to grasp for an alternative vision of his own, and he too began to advocate radical solutions to the problems of racism, poverty and war. King's critique of capitalism, which had been present even before the Montgomery Bus Boycott, now grew stronger:

"Why are there 40 million poor people in America? And when you begin to ask that question, you are raising a question about the economic system, about a broader distribution of wealth. When you ask that question, you begin to question the capitalistic economy. And I'm simply saying that more and more, we've got to begin to ask questions about the whole society. We are called upon to help the discouraged beggars in life's marketplace. But one day we must come to see that an edifice which produces beggars needs restructuring." (West, p171-2)

King had been arguing for a Poor People's Campaign which could unite black and white people since 1966 but he now fleshed out those ideas. Thousands of poor people from across the country should descend on the capital and demand a radical Economic Bill of Rights, he said. And King's language increasingly shifted from talk of "reform" to talk of "revolution". Issuing a radical challenge to those leading the Black Power charge, he wrote, "To dislocate the functioning of a city without destroying it can be more effective than a riot because it can be longer-lasting... Moreover, it is more difficult for the government to quell it by superior force...we will have to develop mass disciplined forces that can remain excited and determined without dramatic conflagrations." (Martin Luther King, *The Crisis in America's Cities*, SCLC, August 15, 1967, p6)

But as King began to advocate "Poor People's Power", his allies in the SCLC were aghast. The majority of his organisation consisted of religious figures from the South, and most were from comfortable middle class backgrounds. King's call to engage in a form of class struggle was not something many knew how to swallow even if they wanted to. Even trusted lieutenants, such as Jesse Jackson, felt the SCLC had other priorities. The plan faced further difficulties. The SCLC had few relations with the white working class, North or South, and no one experienced in labour organising. There was no specific plan for how to overcome the racial prejudices that many whites harboured. Given the obstacles, how were the SCLC supposed to mobilise tens of thousands to come to Washington and engage in radical action? Faced with these questions, King struggled for answers.

He had already ruffled feathers, but it was King's decision to speak out publicly against America's increasing involvement in Vietnam that really shocked both white liberals and his long-time supporters. Opposition to the war was still in 1967 politically marginal, confined to some students and radicals. In the most politically charged speech of his life, King opened saying, there comes a time when "silence is betrayal", and went on to tear the case for war into pieces. He finished calling for an end to the "giant triplets of racism, extreme materialism, and militarism".

The bringing together of opposition to the war, the fight against racism and the battle against poverty meant King had thrown down the gauntlet to the whole system, and the system responded in the only way it knew how. The *Washington Post* talked of his "sheer inventions of unsupported fantasy" and bemoaned how "many who have listened to him with respect will never again accord him the same confidence." The *New York Times* called King's remarks both "facile" and "slander". Even some of the black-owned press joined the attack.

The FBI, which already had a 17,000-page file on King, went into overdrive. In 1968 Bureau analysts described him as a "a whole-hearted Marxist who has studied it (Marxism), believes in it and agrees with it, but because of his being a minister of religion, does not dare to espouse it publicly". King, they insisted, was a communist who followed a "Marxist-Leninist line". The FBI used their vast network of informers to spread stories and

KING ON VIETNAM

"Over the past two years, as I have moved to break the betrayal of my own silences and to speak from the burnings of my own heart, as I have called for radical departures from the destruction of Vietnam, many persons have questioned me about the wisdom of my path. At the heart of their concerns, this query has often loomed large and loud: 'Why are you speaking about the war, Dr King? Why are you joining the voices of dissent?' 'Peace and civil rights don't mix,' they say. 'Aren't you hurting the cause of your people?' they ask. And when I hear them, though I often understand the source of their concern, I am nevertheless greatly saddened, for such questions mean that the inquirers have not really known me, my commitment, or my calling. Indeed, their questions suggest that they do not know the world in which they live."

"As I have walked among the desperate, rejected, and angry young men, I have told them that Molotov cocktails and rifles would not solve their problems... But they asked, and rightly so, 'What about Vietnam?' They asked if our own nation wasn't using massive doses of violence to solve its problems, to bring about the changes it wanted. Their questions hit home, and I knew that I could never again raise my voice against the violence of the oppressed in the ghettos without having first spoken clearly to the greatest purveyor of violence in the world today: my own government."

rumours against him in the movement and in the media. They helped ensure that funding for his Poor People's Campaign dried up and that his supporters were put on the defensive.

While his political stance was attacked by liberals and the right, King knew that to galvanise radical support he needed more than words; he needed action. But with his organisational apparatus in pieces and fighting among itself, where would the impetus come from? The answer came from an unlikely source—a strike by refuse workers from Memphis, Tennessee.

On a rainy day in February 1968 Echol Cole and Robert Walker sought shelter in the back of their rubbish truck as it rolled down Colonial Street. An electrical short-circuit started the hydraulic ram into action and the two black men were crushed with the putrefying waste—like so much garbage. Nearly the entirety of the 1,300 Memphis sanitation workers, all of them black, immediately walked out on strike. Tensions had been brewing since the early 1960s when a group of trade unionists started a drive for recognition, decent pay, protective clothing and better safety on the job.

In the Memphis strike King saw the possibility of reviving his Poor People's Campaign. It must have occurred to him that, rather than try to organise workers from the outside, what if they could organise themselves? The strikers readily identified themselves with the Civil Rights Movement and wore placards saying, "I AM A MAN". King addressed them and their supporters in one of the largest indoor mass rallies of the civil rights era. He celebrated their resistance, saying, "You are reminding, not only Memphis, but you are reminding the nation that it is a crime for people to live in this rich nation and receive starvation wages. And I need not remind you that this is our plight as a people all over America." The best way for workers to fight poverty, King said, is a union. (West, 2015, p246)

But in this improvised speech, he went further still, saying:

"Don't go back on the job until the demands are met. Never forget that freedom is not something that is voluntarily given by the oppressor. It is something that must be demanded by the oppressed. Freedom is not some lavish dish that the power structure and the white forces in policy-making positions will voluntarily hand out on a silver platter while the Negro merely furnishes the appetite. If we are going to get equality, if we are going to get adequate wages, we are going to have to struggle for it.

Now you know what? You may have to escalate the struggle a bit. If they keep refusing, and they will not recognise the union, and will not agree for the check-off for the collection of dues, I tell you what you ought to do, and you are together here enough to do it—in a few days you ought to get together and just have a general work stoppage in the city of Memphis." (West, 2015, p246)

King then promised to return to Memphis and lead a huge march through the city. The minister, who started his political life in the fight for desegregated buses 13 years earlier, was now a bitter opponent of the government and its foreign wars and was calling for a city-wide general strike. He, and the ideas he embodied, had travelled a long way. And the more radical he became, the more of a threat the US establishment and its allies calculated him to be. King was often singled out for physical attack while marching, and when his plane to Memphis was disrupted by a bomb threat, few were surprised.

King did return to the city and its strikers to address a mass meeting on the night of 3 April 1968. Midway through his speech, to the consternation of his audience and staff, King broke off and started speaking of himself in the past tense, saying, "Well, I don't know what will happen now. We've got some difficult days ahead. But it really doesn't matter with me now, because I've been to the mountaintop. And I don't mind. Like anybody, I would like to live a long life—longevity has its place. But I'm not concerned about that now. I just want to do God's will. And He's allowed me to go up to the mountain. And I've looked over. And I've seen the Promised Land. I may not get there with you. But I want you to know tonight, that we, as a people, will get to the Promised Land."

The next day, at 6.08pm, on the balcony of the Lorraine Hotel in Memphis, King was shot and killed by a white racist, James Earl Ray.

★ 11: AFTER MARTIN

The riots that swept America in the wake of King's assassination were the greatest wave of civil unrest the country had experienced since the Civil War. Washington sent troops to the main cities, while Mayor Daley in Chicago, who had so vigorously opposed King's campaign in his city two years earlier, gave the order to shoot on sight anyone suspected of looting. No one knows what the final death toll in the city was because no one was keeping count.

Two key political strands emerged in the fight for black liberation in the wake of King's death, though it was not always easy to see their differing directions at the time. A new, radical left developed primarily out of the struggle against the war but which readily embraced the spirit of Black Power. Led by students who rejected both capitalism and Soviet Communism, they searched for inspiration from Mao's China, Third World freedom movements in Africa and Asia, and from the ghetto uprisings closer to home. The Black Panthers' meteoric rise from a couple of California students to a nationwide movement with a base in the ghettos and support among young white radicals is one of many examples of the forms rebellion took.

But another is the growth of the black middle class, and from them, the black elected official. The battles of the Civil Rights Movement, combined with the threat of further urban uprisings, created the space for a buffer layer of black politicians who generally came from a radical background. They sought to divert the anger that burned in US cities into social programmes—and, crucially, the ballot box. Yet, despite many a city electing black mayors, and them in turn appointing black police chiefs and other black officials, the pace of change in the ghetto remained pitifully slow or non-existent.

In the mid-1970s, as recession gripped the world economy, life for Americans trapped in the corners of the city went from bad to worse. Unemployment skyrocketed, slum housing deteriorated into wrecks and life became unbearable for millions, with the increasing use of hard drugs one of many consequences. With no money available, the city authorities could do nothing but insist on repeated "law and order" crackdowns, and more racist policing.

But the forces that once stood up to the cops were by now a shadow of their former selves. Police repression and internal divisions smashed the Panthers, and the once young anti-war radicals were jaded and without hope. When Gil Scott-Heron, the radical rap pioneer, wrote his album *Winter in America* he was not lost for themes. For those that continued to identify the system as the generator of oppression, the question of what force could defeat it was vital, but it seemed that no one had the answer.

The idea that King had stumbled upon in Memphis— that working class people could play the key role in the fight for liberation—was rejected by most radicals and the New Left as an ideological hangover, despite this being a period of intense class warfare in the factories and beyond.

★ 12
CONCLUSION

The racial flaws of capitalist societies are in some ways clearer now than they were in King's time. Fifty years after his assassination US society, North and South, still burns with injustice but there is now no insisting that the malady is confined to only the Southern part of the country. From the regularity of murderous police brutality to the president's support for white supremacist demonstrations in Charlottesville in 2017, for many it seems as if progress is being rolled backwards, that gains once made are being washed away. What is true of the US is also obvious elsewhere. Islamophobia, a form of racism with a "respectable" veneer, has spread across the globe. Contempt for refugees in Europe has turned the Mediterranean into a sea of death for those attempting to escape war and poverty.

The contours and patterns of racial prejudice differ in each epoch, each country and each continent, making direct historical comparisons with the story of the Civil Rights Movement difficult and sometimes unhelpful. Nevertheless, the conclusions that King arrived at towards the end of his life have enduring relevance. The understanding that racism, poverty and war are inevitable features of capitalism led King to consider what kind of society a truly liberated humanity would build.

His conclusions on this were sometimes vague and unclear, as though he was still working his way through the problem at the point of his premature end. But it is clear from King's writing and speaking that he did not believe the solution lay in merely "putting black faces in high places". That would only entail a changing of the guard when something far more fundamental was required. The huge increase in the number of black elected officials during the 1970s and 80s was ultimately capped by the election of Barak Obama as US president in 2008 and 2012. The election of the first black president of the US was celebrated as millions projected their hopes for change onto Obama. But on so many measures, Obama failed. The racial gap continued to widen in his eight years as black median income fell by 10.9 percent compared to 3.6 percent for whites. And the militarism that King had warned about was barely constrained in this period, with Obama ordering ten times more drone strikes under his presidency than his predecessor, George W Bush.

King did not think that more laws would by themselves bring substantive change. Instead he was looking for a way to mobilise millions of people—and change their hearts and minds in the process. He wanted to break the hold of racist ideas, yes, but also to break the hold of a minority of powerful people upon the majority, black and white.

King's attachment to the Memphis sanitation strike was symbolic, not only because these overwhelmingly black workers were at the very bottom of society, but because it proved that even those at the bottom had potential power, an economic and social muscle that they could flex. In the process of this kind of struggle, workers learn quickly who their friends and enemies are, and how to win over waverers. They learn the power of the state and the media, but also arrive at creative means of overcoming them. Crucially, examples of working class resistance can readily spread to millions of others who face similarly brutal exploitation. Class struggle is about more than seeking some form of economic and social justice, it also has the potential to break the hold of long-held prejudices and hatreds. It was precisely this understanding that led the ruling class of the South to erect the walls of segregation in the first place.

This project for radical change can rely on no easy solutions or quick fixes. Prejudice has been cultivated by our rulers for generations since slavery. Today's racism is a cancer in the working class movement that eats away at the ties of solidarity, it feeds on the anxieties that all too often dominate people's lives, and the resulting lack of confidence can in turn deepen the hold of backward ideas. But this vicious cycle can be broken. Millions of people in Britain, and across the world, reject racism and want real change. Many have donated to refugee collections, signed petitions, stood up for colleagues and friends, gone to meetings and joined protests. One of our tasks must be to build a movement capable of uniting everyone who opposes bigotry—and, in that, we can take great inspiration from King and the Civil Rights Movement.

But we must also seek to answer King's question about what kind of society could replace capitalism by arguing and fighting for the alternative—socialism. In King's time the ideas of the radical left were very much tainted by the Cold War, and the Stalinism of the Soviet Union. The genuine socialist tradition is far from the caricatures of the time—instead it is about human liberation, the possibility of constructing a world without races, nations and walls.

Such a world can only come about through revolution.

★ READ ON

General histories of American racism and the Civil Rights Movement

Jack M Bloom, *Class, race and the civil rights movement*
(Indiana University Press, 1987)

Clayborne Carson et al (eds) *The eyes on the prize civil rights reader: documents, speeches and firsthand accounts from the black freedom struggle, 1954-1990* (Penguin, 1992)

Manning Marable, *Race, reform and rebellion: the Second Reconstruction and beyond in Black America, 1945-2006* (University Press of Mississippi, 2007)

Brian Richardson (ed), S*ay it loud: Marxism and the fight against racism* (Bookmarks, 2013). See in particular my chapter on the history of the fight against racism in the United States

Ahmed Shawki, *Black liberation and socialism* (Haymarket Books, 2006)

On Martin Luther King specifically

Vincent Harding, *Martin Luther King: The Inconvenient Hero*
(Orbis, 2008)

Brian Kelly, *Unfinished business: Martin Luther King in Memphis*
(International Socialism journal, 2008)
isj.org.uk/unfinished-business-martin-luther-king-in-memphis/

Cornell West (ed), *The Radical King* (Beacon Press, 2015)

Gary Younge, *The Speech: The Story Behind Martin Luther King's Dream* (Haymarket, 2013)

King in his own words

Most of Martin Luther King's speeches are available online. Wikipedia has a dedicated page of his sermons and speeches with useful links. Of his many books, I recommend starting with his 1968 classic, *Where Do We Go From Here? Chaos or Community* (Beacon Press, 2010).

Martin Luther King, Jr, *Autobiography* (Abacus, 2000)

Martin Luther King, Jr, *Stride toward freedom, the Montgomery story* (Souvenir Press, 2010)

More Bookmarks Rebel's Guides

A Rebel's Guide to James Connolly by Seán Mitchell

A Rebel's Guide to Eleanor Marx by Siobhan Brown

A Rebel's Guide to Rosa Luxemburg by Sally Campbell

A Rebel's Guide to Gramsci by Chris Bambery

A Rebel's Guide to Trotsky by Esme Choonara

A Rebel's Guide to Marx by Mike Gonzalez

A Rebel's Guide to Lenin by Ian Birchall

A Rebel's Guide to Malcolm X by Antony Hamilton

Sexism and the System: A Rebel's Guide to Women's Liberation
    by Judith Orr

Available from Bookmarks, 1 Bloomsbury Street, London WC1B 3QE
info@bookmarksbookshop.co.uk bookmarksbookshop.co.uk
020 7637 1848

★ LISTEN

A Spotify and Apple Music playlist to accompany this book is available. Search Rebel's Guide to Martin Luther King to listen while you read.